CHINESE AND JAPANESE MYTHS

By Jen Green

Gareth Stevens
Publishing

Please visit our Web site www.garethstevens.com. For a free color catalog of all our high-quality books, call toll free 1-800-542-2595 or fax 1-877-542-2596.

Library of Congress Cataloging-in-Publication Data
Green, Jen.
   Chinese and Japanese myths / Jen Green.
      p. cm. -- (Myths from around the world)
   Includes index.
   ISBN 978-1-4339-3533-6 (library binding) -- ISBN 978-1-4339-3534-3 (pbk.)
   ISBN 978-1-4339-3535-0 (library binding)
   1. Mythology, Chinese--Juvenile literature. 2. Mythology, Japanese--Juvenile literature.   I. Title.
   BL1825.G735 2010
   398.20951--dc22   2009039330

Published in 2010 by
Gareth Stevens Publishing
111 East 14th Street, Suite 349
New York, NY 10003

© 2010 The Brown Reference Group Ltd.

For Gareth Stevens Publishing:
Art Direction: Haley Harasymiw
Editorial Direction: Kerri O'Donnell

For The Brown Reference Group Ltd:
Editorial Director: Lindsey Lowe
Managing Editor: Tim Cooke
Editor: Henry Russell
Children's Publisher: Anne O'Daly
Picture Manager: Sophie Mortimer
Design Manager: David Poole
Designers: Tim Mayer and John Walker
Production Director: Alastair Gourlay

Picture Credits:
Front Cover: Shutterstock: Eastimages t; Mumbojumbo br; Surabky b

iStock: Japanthings 32; G.D. Pozzi 40; Sack 29t; Sosb 29b; Jan Tyler 44; Zaricm 45t;
Jupiter Images: AbleStock 14/15; Photos.com 7, 41t, 45b; Stockxpert 24, 33t;
Shutterstock: 36; Maxim Amelin; Henrik Anderson 5; Thomas Barrat 21; Sandra Caldwell 9; Christopher Meder Photography 13t; Jeroen De Mast 16; Zhu Difeng 4; Ikya D. Gridbev 39; Craig Hanson 37; Hiroshi Ichikawa 28; Jorisro 20; Ingvald Kaldhussater 33b; John Lock 11; Luftikus 43; Xi Leo 17t; Antonio M. Magdaraog 17b; Martine Oger 8; Open Best Design Stock 25; PapiMami 23; Romasan 41b; Samkin 19; Michael Schofield 35; Timage 12, 13b; Tororo Reaction 27

Publisher's note to educators and parents: Our editors have carefully reviewed the Web sites that appear on p. 47 to ensure that they are suitable for students. Many Web sites change frequently, however, and we cannot guarantee that a site's future contents will continue to meet our high standards of quality and educational value. Be advised that students should be closely supervised whenever they access the Internet.

Manufactured in the United States of America
1 2 3 4 5 6 7 8 9 12 11 10

0143

CPSIA compliance information: Batch #BRW0102GS: For further information contact Gareth Stevens, New York, New York at 1-800-542-2595.

Contents

Introduction 4

The Story of Creation 6

Chinese Religions 8

August Personage of Jade 10

Dynastic China 12

The Excellent Archer 14

Climate and Farming in China 16

How Yu Tamed the Waters 18

China's Great Rivers 20

Empress of Heaven 22

Ships and Seafaring 24

The Creation of Japan 26

The Japanese Islands 28

Izanagi Visits the Underworld 30

Religion in Japan 32

Amaterasu Hides the Daylight 34

Farming in Japan 36

Susano-wo and the Dragon's Sword 38

Swords and Samurai 40

Okuninushi and Ninigi 42

The Emperors of Japan 44

Glossary and Further Information 46

Index 48

Introduction

Myths are mirrors of humanity. They reflect the soul of a culture and try to give profound answers in a seemingly mysterious world. They give the people an understanding of their place in the world and the universe.

Found in all civilizations, myths sometimes combine fact and fiction and, at other times, are complete fantasy.

Every culture has its own myths. Yet, globally, there are common themes, even across civilizations that had no contact with each other. The most common myths deal with the creation of the world or of a particular site, like a mountain or a lake. Other myths deal with the origin of humans or describe the heroes and gods who either made the world inhabitable or who provided humans with something essential, such as the ancient Greek Titan Prometheus, who gave fire, and the

Confucius (551–479 B.C.) was a great influence on Chinese religion.

Native American Wunzh, who was given divine instructions on cultivating corn. There are also myths about the end of the world, death, and the afterlife.

The origin of evil and death are also common themes. Examples of such myths are the Biblical Eve eating the forbidden fruit and the ancient Greek story of Pandora opening the sealed box. Additionally, there are flood myths, myths about the sun and the moon, and myths of peaceful places of reward, such as heaven or Elysium, and of places of punishment, such as hell or Tartarus. Myths also teach human values, such as courage and honesty.

This book features some

of the most important ancient Chinese and Japanese myths. Following each myth is an explanation of how the myth related to real life. A glossary at the end of the book identifies the major mythological and historical characters and explains many cultural terms.

Mythology of China and Japan

Historians believe that ancient Chinese mythology began around the twelfth century B.C. For more than 1,000 years afterward, all the myths were passed down by word of mouth from generation to generation. Eventually the ancient myths became assimilated into the religious tales of the three major belief systems: Confucianism, Taoism, and Buddhism. In general, the supreme deity of Chinese mythology was the Jade Emperor. He ruled over a large bureaucratic network of lesser deities whose responsibilities included running day-to-day administrative affairs on earth. This complicated structure in heaven actually imitated the real bureaucracy that existed in the Chinese emperor's imperial court.

Many ancient Chinese myths and mythological characters were influential in the development of the mythology of Japan, several hundred miles to the east.

Images of Buddha are found throughout Japan. This giant statue is in Kamakura, near Tokyo.

However, Shinto, the ancient religion of Japan, was unique to the island nation. Its mythology centers around Amaterasu, the sun goddess. Shinto stresses the harmony of humans with nature. There is an infinite number of deities and spirits, called *kami*, that are believed to exist in all kinds of inanimate objects of nature, from rocks to streams. Some *kami* come from the souls of the dead, and eventually all souls become *kami*. In addition to the stories of Amaterasu and the other major deities, the adventures of the *kami* form the majority of Japanese myths.

The Story of Creation

In the beginning, only a confused, misty nothingness existed. It was shaped like an enormous egg. Gradually, a giant called Pan Ku emerged out of the nothingness.

Pan Ku decided to create the universe, so he made an ax and struck the egg-shaped mass, splitting it in two. All the dark, heavy forces of the mass, called the yin, sank down to become the earth, and all the bright, light elements, called the yang, rose up to become the heavens.

Fearing that the two halves of his creation would merge back into one, Pan Ku planted his feet firmly on the earth and pushed the heavens farther upward. For 18,000 years, the giant kept pushing, until the earth and the heavens were finally fixed in place. When Pan Ku died, his body changed to become the outer layer of the world as we know it. His back became the rugged mountains, and his blood became the seas and rivers. His breath turned into the wind, and plants sprouted from his skin. His hair flew high into the heavens and became the twinkling stars.

Now more gods and goddesses came into being, but there were no humans. Humans were the work of a goddess named Nu Wa. Nu Wa's upper body looked human, but she had a serpent's tail. The goddess roamed the earth and found it beautiful but lonely.

Clay Figures

On the banks of the Yellow River in China, Nu Wa scooped up clay and fashioned it into a tiny figure. The top half of the figure resembled the upper part of the goddess's body, but the lower half had two legs instead of Nu Wa's serpent's tail. The goddess stood the figure on the bank and breathed life into it. Immediately it started laughing and dancing for joy.

Nu Wa made more people in the same way, but the work was slow and laborious. She then took a vine, dipped it in mud, and whirled it around in a large circle. Each drop of mud that fell to the ground became a person. Some say that the humans Nu Wa made by hand became rich and fortunate, and the drops of mud became all the world's poor people.

South Korea's flag features the yin–yang symbol (the red and blue circle) and four trigrams representing the Chinese principles of harmony, symmetry, balance, and circulation.

Chinese Religions

Three major belief systems, or religions, evolved in China. In general, these religions do not compete with each other. Instead, the Chinese practice whatever elements of the major religions feel most suitable.

Archaeologists believe that Chinese civilization began around 3000 B.C. on the banks of the Yellow River (also known as the Huang Ho)—the site where Nu Wa made her clay figures—in northeastern China. The local people, called the Han, grew crops in the river valley, and built first villages, then towns, along the riverbanks. Civilization gradually spread southward across the neighboring plain to another valley, along the Yangtze River (also called the Cheng). The land of China came to be called *Zhong-guo* ("Middle Kingdom"), because the Chinese believed that it lay at the center of the world.

Chinese Belief Systems

Beginning some 2,500 years ago, three religions, or ways of living, took root in China: Buddhism, Confucianism, and Taoism. Most Chinese gods and goddesses are of Taoist origin, but some myths draw on different beliefs. Confucianism, which is more a cultural approach to life than a set of spiritual beliefs, was founded by the philosopher K'ung Fu-tzu, better known as Confucius (551–479 B.C.). Mainly concerned with practical matters and maintaining a high moral order within society, Confucianism stresses the importance of respecting one's ancestors, tradition, and the law.

Chinese religions are based more on philosophies than on mysticism.

Taoism, founded around the same time as Confucianism, is a mystical religion. Followers of the Tao (which means "the way" and stands for the creation of everything) strive for perfection through harmony with nature and by balancing the forces of yin and yang. The teachings of the religion are based on two key texts, *Tao-te Ching* and *Chuang Tzu*. The most important Taoist myths come from two other books, *Travels in the West* and *Romance of the Investiture of the Gods*. Both these books were written during the Ming dynasty in the fifteenth century A.D.

The third major philosophical or religious movement, Buddhism, began in India in the fifth century B.C. and reached China some 2,000 years ago. Today there are some 300 million Buddhists around the world. In China, Buddhism remains influential in part because it offers a belief that souls are reincarnated after death. The moral law called karma teaches that people who live especially virtuous lives are reborn in higher forms, while those who live sinful lives are reborn in lower forms.

The goddess of mercy, Quan Yin, is worshipped by Buddhists and Taoists in China and Japan.

YIN AND YANG

Taoists believe that two opposite and equal forces, yin and yang, underlie everything in the universe, with each containing the potential to create the other. Yin is considered cool, moist, dark, and feminine; yang is warm, dry, bright, and male. Yang can control yin when it grows dangerously excessive. In the creation story (see page 6), yin represents earth and yang stands for heaven. Together they create a balanced harmony.

August Personage of Jade

Yu Huang Shang-di is the most important Chinese god and ruler of the heavens. His name means "the August Personage of Jade," and he is also known as the Jade Emperor.

There are several versions of the origin of Yu Huang, the Jade Emperor. According to some versions, he was one of the first gods to have existed. In other accounts, he was one of three supreme deities. One legend states that he was born after his mother had a vision in which a holy man called Lao-tzu (a real person who is credited with founding the Taoist religion, see page 8) handed her a child. In that same myth, Yu Huang grew up to become a king, but later stepped down from his throne to study religion. As a holy man, he attained perfection and at the moment of his death became an immortal god. Millions of years later, he transformed into the Jade Emperor.

As the Jade Emperor, Yu Huang lived in the most beautiful palace in the highest level of heaven. He had a long wispy beard and wore a crown topped with a flat board hung with strings of pearls. His robes were embroidered with imperial dragons and he sat on a large throne.

Yu Huang was married to Xi Wangmu, who was also known as the Queen Mother of the West. Young and beautiful, she was often accompanied by a peacock. In her garden, she grew a magical peach tree that bore fruit only once every 3,000 years. When the fruit ripened, the Queen Mother would host a banquet for the gods at which the peaches were the main food. The magic peaches gave the gods immortality.

Divine Hierarchy

As ruler of the heavens, the Jade Emperor was too busy and important to have any direct involvement with affairs on earth.

Instead he oversaw thousands of lesser gods and goddesses who were responsible for looking after the world and its inhabitants. Some deities were nature spirits in charge of lakes, rivers, and mountains. Other deities were patrons of particular activities and professions. For example, young men trying to pass the exams that led to lucrative administration careers with the imperial court prayed to K'uei Hsing, the god of examinations. There were also gods and goddesses who governed happiness, mercy, good fortune, and long life.

Gods had to report to their superiors once a month, and to the Jade Emperor once a year. If a deity's conduct was unsatisfactory, he could be dismissed and replaced by another god. Thus, over time, many divine offices were held by several gods.

The clothing and style of Yu Huang, the Jade Emperor, were copied by the Chinese emperors on earth.

Dynastic China

The Chinese believed that their emperors were appointed by heaven. As long as they ruled justly, their positions were safe and their authority was total, but if they failed, they could be deposed.

Early Chinese emperors took the title "Sons of Heaven" and modeled their courts on the heavenly court of the Jade Emperor (see page 10). The emperor was believed to be a deity on earth whose word was law. If, however, an emperor failed in his duties, he would lose the mandate of heaven and could be replaced by another nobleman who would begin a new dynasty. Dynasties were periods of rule by a particular family.

The Shang were China's first great dynasty. They ruled northeastern China from 1650 B.C. to 1027 B.C. They were followed by the Zhou (1027–256 B.C.), who established a feudal system in which ordinary people were ruled by overlords. The Zhou era ended after a civil war, and the Ch'in dynasty (221–207 B.C.), led by Emperor Cheng (259–210 B.C.), reunited the country.

Cheng, who called himself Shih Huang-ti, which means "First Sovereign Emperor," began work on the Great Wall. The wall, which marks China's northern boundary and stretches 4,000 miles (6,400 km), was intended to keep out invaders.

During the Han dynasty (207 B.C–A.D. 220), the emperors strengthened their control over China. They established a civil service, which governed the empire for the next 2,000 years.

The terra-cotta army, consisting of more than 8,000 life-size figures, was made by craftspeople during the reign of the emperor Cheng, the first ruler of a unified China.

dynasty (1368–1644), which was eventually replaced by the Qing in 1682.

After a long period of unrest, the Sui ruled China from A.D. 589 to 618. Their greatest achievement was the canal that links the Yangtze and Yellow rivers.

During the Tang dynasty (618–906), China's economy prospered, and literature and music flourished. The Song dynasty (960–1279) oversaw many advances in technology. Trade boomed under the Yuan (or Mongol) dynasty (1279–1368). After the Yuan came the Ming

The End of the Empire

By the beginning of the 20th century, imperial rule had been fatally weakened. In 1912, the Qing dynasty and imperial rule in China ended when the Chinese military set up a republic.

The imperial palace in Beijing was the seat of Chinese government and the hub of political power.

The Excellent Archer

According to an ancient Chinese myth, the heroic Yi, the divine archer, was the only being powerful enough to prevent the ten suns from burning the crops.

Long ago, the earth had not one sun but ten suns. The suns were the children of the god Di Jun and his wife Xi He. Together they lived in the branches of a giant mulberry tree in the east. Each morning, one of the suns would rise and set off across the heavens, leaving his nine brothers in the tree. The next day, another sun would cross the sky. On earth, people thought there was only one sun.

After a thousand years of taking turns, the suns rebelled and all rose into the sky at once. On earth, temperatures grew hotter and hotter. Rivers dried up and rocks melted. Worst of all, the crops withered.

Yao, emperor of China, went to Di Jun and pleaded with him to recall his sons. "My people will starve unless you help us," the emperor cried. Di Jun summoned the divine archer, Yi, and asked him to deal with the problem.

He gave Yi a strong bow and a quiver with 10 arrows—one for each sun.

Yi climbed a high crag and warned the suns to return home, but they took no notice. As they climbed higher in the sky, plains and forests were singed bare, and the land itself began to burn.

Sharpshooter

Yi strung his bow and fired an arrow straight at a sun. It exploded in a burst of light and fell to earth. Now Yi released a volley of arrows. One by one, the suns fell, and temperatures grew cooler on earth. Fearful that all the suns would die, the emperor crept up behind Yi and stole one of his arrows. When Yi's quiver was empty, one sun still remained in the sky to give light to the world.

Di Jun was filled with sorrow at the death of his nine sons. Even though

The ten suns withered the crops and threatened to scorch the land. Yi shot down nine of them, leaving one to provide the right amount of sunlight.

he had asked Yi to help, he now banished him and his wife, Zhang E, to earth. He condemned them to live and die like ordinary mortals. In despair, Yi went to Xi Wangmu, Queen Mother of the West, and asked for her help. Taking pity on him, the supreme goddess gave him the potion of immortality, which was made from her magic peaches. She told him to share it with his wife.

Yi returned home and told Zhang E the good news. When he went out again, his wife drank all the potion. The dose was too strong for one person and Zhang E's body became lighter than air. She floated upward all the way to the moon, where she now lives with a divine hare. You can still see Zhang E's hare if you look up at the full moon.

Climate and Farming in China

As the world's most populous country, China depends on the success of its agriculture. Throughout history, the country's farmers have had to battle extreme weather conditions.

Today over a billion people live in China. Historically the country has always been heavily populated. With so many mouths to feed, farming has been a great priority. A disaster like the drought caused by the ten suns (see page 14) would have threatened China's people with famine.

In 111 B.C., Emperor Wu Di declared, "Agriculture is the foundation of the world," and decreed that farmers should be respected. Even so, the farming life was still hard. Farmers toiled in the fields from dawn till dusk, yet had to pay taxes and join the army in wartime. They also had to help with projects such as building public roads and waterways.

Despite China's enormous size, only a relatively small part of the country is fertile farmland. In ancient times, eastern China was the most densely populated region because it was the

The Chinese have grown and harvested rice in the same way for centuries.

most fertile. Farmers there cut steps of terraces into steep hillsides to make the most of what land there was, and spread ash and manure to fertilize the fields.

Range of Crops

Rice is one of the main food crops in China, but it requires warm, wet growing conditions. In the humid south, it has been cultivated for over 6,000 years. Barley, wheat, and millet were grown in the yellow soil of the north. Hemp, cotton, tea, and fruits such as oranges, pears, litchi nuts, and cherries were also

Terraces used for rice paddies have been cut into mountainsides throughout China.

Sheep were also important to Chinese farmers as a source of meat and wool.

cultivated. Farmers kept pigs, ducks, geese, and chickens, and reared silkworms for silk.

Early Chinese farmers worked with simple tools, such as hoes, rakes, and sickles. By the fifth century B.C., oxen and buffalo were used to pull iron plows. In the second century A.D., better horse harnesses were invented. Around the same time, farmers began to transport their goods to market by wheelbarrow.

During this era, the Chinese invented new machines, including pedal hammers for husking, water-driven hammers in mills, hand-powered sifting or winnowing machines, and watermills for grinding grain.

How Yu Tamed the Waters

Emperor Yao's long reign was troubled with many problems. After Yi had rid the earth of the rebellious suns, another powerful god, Tiandi, sent Gonggong to destroy mankind.

Tiandi, one of the gods of heaven, grew tired of human wickedness. He ordered Gonggong, the god of water, to cause a great flood that would drown all the people. When the floods began, Yao called on the gods to save his people. Gun, a god who often took the form of a white horse, heard the emperor's prayer.

Gun wandered the earth, trying to find a way of controlling the rising waters. He met with an owl and a tortoise, who told him about a magic clay that would swell up when it came in contact with water. They suggested that the magic clay could be used to build a dam.

The clay was carefully guarded, but after many adventures, Gun finally succeeded in stealing enough of it to build a giant dam that soon held the floods in check. When Tiandi saw what Gun had done, he became angry. He sent down a fire god who killed Gun and wrecked the dam. The floodwaters breached the barrier and surged back over the land.

Stemming the Flood

Still Gun's desire to help humankind was so strong that out of his body his son, Yu, was born. Yu, who could take the form of a dragon, continued his father's work. He plugged the 233,599 springs from which the floodwaters gushed. For 13 years he traveled the kingdom, marking out the boundaries of China's nine provinces. Tiandi saw his efforts and, at last, he allowed Yu to defeat Gonggong.

Using his dragon's tail, Yu gouged a series of deep furrows into the earth. These channels became China's great rivers, which discharged the floodwaters

into the sea. Yu then showed the people how to use the magic clay to build great dams and dikes that would protect low-lying areas from flooding.

In later years, Yu married but did not tell his wife he was a god. One day, seeing him in the form of a bear, she died of fright. It was then that her son, Qi, was born from her body. Qi grew up to become one of China's wisest and mightiest emperors.

The god Yu used his magic powers to stop the floodwaters from covering the world. For the Chinese, floods from mighty rivers, such as this, have always been real threats.

China's Great Rivers

Myths about great floods that cover the earth are a feature of many different cultures. The Chinese had particular reason to fear the destructive power of floods.

The Yellow and Yangtze are the two greatest rivers in eastern China. The Yellow River flows across northern China. The Yangtze divides the cool, dry north of China from the green, humid south.

Archaeologists believe that, around 3000 B.C., the valleys of these two great rivers were the birthplace of Chinese civilization. The ancient Chinese settled along the rivers because the soil there was ideal for farming. From time to time after heavy rain, the rivers burst their banks and spilled out over the surrounding plains. When the waters subsided, a rich, deep layer of fertile soil was left for farmers to cultivate crops.

During drier periods, the ancient Chinese peasants used river water to irrigate their fields and terraced hillsides. From around A.D. 1100, water was raised using a type of human-powered treadmill called an endless wheel. The endless wheel was operated by peasants who stood atop a large cogwheel and trod on pedals that turned the wheel and pumped water

The world's longest artificial waterway, the Grand Canal, is both a major transportation artery and a source of water for some of the drier regions of China.

BUILDING FLOOD DEFENSES

Throughout China's long history, successive emperors built dams and high dikes to control rivers. The river channels were also dredged to make them deeper, but to little effect. The flood defenses were always breached by the rivers at high water. Today a major new dam system, called the Three Gorges project, is underway on the Yangtze River. A new, giant dam protects the valley from flooding and will generate hydroelectricity. More than a million people have had to abandon their homes to make way for the huge reservoir that has been created by the new dam.

upward. The Yangtze and Yellow rivers also acted as routes for shipping and were prime spots for fishing.

The Chinese then built a network of waterways to extend the natural river systems. In the sixth century A.D., during the Sui dynasty, a great canal was built to link the Yangtze River and the Yellow River. The Grand Canal took 30 years to complete. During its construction, all men in China between the ages of 15 and 50 had to help with the digging. The finished canal stretched for 1,550 miles (2,500 km).

China's Sorrow

The Yangtze River and the Yellow River brought many blessings, but also terrible destruction. When the rivers burst their banks and floodwater surged over the lowlands, whole towns and villages were swept away and thousands of people were drowned. The Yellow River was particularly treacherous, and even today it is known as "China's Sorrow," because of its terrible history of flooding. In 1938, a major flood from the river killed nearly one million people.

Empress of Heaven

Like the rest of the universe, the seas were under the general authority of the Jade Emperor, but several gods and goddesses protected sailors. The most popular was T'ien Hou, who was also called Empress of Heaven.

Before she became a goddess, T'ien Hou had been human. As a little girl, she lived on the island of Mei-chou. She had four brothers, who were all fishermen. One day each of her brothers set out in their own boats to cast their nets in various bays around the island. The young T'ien Hou remained at home.

The brothers had not been gone long when a great storm began brewing on the horizon. As the tempest swirled toward the island, the skies darkened and huge waves crashed down on the little harbor town where T'ien Hou lived with her family. As the storm reached its height, the girl fainted and fell to the ground. Her family tried to rouse her, but without success. Finally T'ien Hou's parents used a potion to wake her. The girl slowly came round. She complained bitterly, saying that she had been woken too soon.

Eventually the storm passed and three of T'ien Hou's brothers sailed back into the harbor. As they scrambled ashore, each told the tale of how he had narrowly escaped death with the help of his little sister. Out at sea, as lightning crashed and thunder roared, giant waves had borne down on the brothers and threatened to swamp their boats. Then, just when each brother thought all was lost, the spirit of T'ien Hou appeared, hovering above the water. Instantly the young girl calmed the waves, saving three of her brothers one after the other.

Lost at Sea

The fourth brother never returned home. He drowned in the tempest because T'ien Hou had been woken before her spirit had time to reach his boat.

A few days later, another storm struck the island. Again T'ien Hou fainted, but this time she could not be roused and she died. Not long afterward, local sailors reported that the girl's spirit had appeared

to save them from the storm. From then on, T'ien Hou's spirit returned to rescue sailors in every storm. As her powers grew, T'ien Hou saved sailors from pirates and even ended droughts by bringing rain. Her fame spread, and she was made first princess, then queen, and finally empress of heaven.

Ships and Seafaring

From early times, the Chinese were a nation of expert sailors. Large and small vessels traveled rivers and coastal waters, braving dangers such as pirates and storms.

The sea goddess is important to the Chinese because the inland waterways and the seas around China have always been used for transportation. Most Chinese boats were small, flat-bottomed, wooden or bamboo craft, such as the sampan, whose name means "three planks." Most Chinese sailors propelled and steered their own crafts with a single oar at the stern.

At sea, larger, stouter craft—as well as the protection of T'ien Hou—were needed to brave rough waters and the fierce tropical storms, called typhoons, that often struck the region. Around A.D. 800, Chinese shipbuilders began to construct large wooden craft with several masts. By medieval times, large, flat-bottomed seafaring ships called junks had been developed. A junk carried up to six masts

Strings of barges, known as river caravans, are a common sight on China's inland waterways.

For centuries Chinese junks were one of the world's largest types of shipping vessels.

with huge, square sails made of woven matting. Below deck, wooden bulkheads divided the ship's hold into compartments. This minimized the effect of leaks and helped the junk to stay afloat if it struck a reef in a storm.

On a visit to China, Italian traveler Marco Polo (1254–1324) was particularly impressed by Chinese junks. Up to 500 feet (150 m) long and 200 feet (60 m) wide, they were five times the size of the largest European vessels of the time. Strong rudders made junks relatively easy to maneuver, even in rough seas.

Exploring the Seas

The Chinese used the compass for navigation long before the Europeans. Invented around A.D. 100, the magnetic compass was not used until around 1000. From then on, it revolutionized navigation for Chinese sailors, who were now able to cross the open oceans, out of sight of land.

Taking advantage of this development, the emperor Yong Le sent a fleet to explore the South China Sea and the Indian Ocean. Led by Admiral Zheng and crewed by 27,000 sailors, the fleet made seven journeys between 1405 and 1433 to Sri Lanka, India, Arabia, and the coast of East Africa.

Later emperors did not share Yong Le's desire to know what lay beyond China's borders. After the fifteenth century, China had little contact with the outside world until the nineteenth century.

The Creation of Japan

The Japanese islands cover millions of square miles off the east coast of Asia. Many Japanese believe their islands were created by a god called Izanagi and his wife, Izanami.

In the beginning, there were seven generations of powerful deities who each created a different part of the heavens and the universe. Izanagi and Izanami were of the youngest generation of gods. They grew up on Takamagahara, also known as the High Plain of Heaven, at a time when most of the universe had been fully formed. Only the earth, which was still unshaped and chaotic, was still to be made. The elder gods asked Izanagi and Izanami to complete the process of creation by molding the earth.

Izanagi and Izanami stood side by side on the floating bridge of heaven, which arched like a giant rainbow toward the unshaped planet, and spent much time contemplating how best to shape the earth. Eventually, Izanagi took the jeweled spear of heaven and dipped it into the misty waters that covered the earth. He stirred the waters several times and then lifted up the heavenly spear. A small drop of water fell from the tip of the spear.

Where it hit, the water thickened and solidified to become the first dry land. The gods named the island Onogoro. Today, several places claim the distinction of being Onogoro, but only the gods know which of Japan's many islands is the real Onogoro.

Gods on Earth

Izanagi and Izanami were so pleased with their creation that they descended to the island to make it their home. They built a house and erected a sacred pillar in honor of the other gods. Next the two gods decided to marry. They began the traditional ceremony by walking around the sacred pillar in opposite directions. After several turns round the pillar, Izanami told her husband that he was the most handsome of all the gods.

Though Izanami was merely paying her husband a compliment, she had broken protocol by speaking first in the marriage ritual—the man, not the woman, is

supposed to speak first on these occasions. Izanami's thoughtlessness angered the other gods. They put a curse on the couple, so that their first offspring was born in the shape of a monstrous leech.

Izanagi and Izanami rejected the leech child, whom they named Hiruko. They abandoned him by casting him adrift in the ocean in a small reed boat. The child survived the dangers of the sea and in time became known as Ebisu, the god of fishermen and good fortune.

After they had sent away the leech child, Izanagi and Izanami became depressed. Taking pity on them, the other gods explained to the couple the mistake

The story of Izanagi and Izanami, the lovers who shaped the earth, reflects the island topography of Japan.

Izanami had made during the wedding ceremony. Now that they fully understood the proper way to perform the ritual, they tried it again. This time they pleased the gods, and the couple's other children were born in more auspicious circumstances. Izanami gave birth to the other islands of Japan, and later to many more deities, including the gods of the wind, the mountains, and the trees.

The Japanese Islands

Japan is made up of four large islands and thousands of small ones in the northwest Pacific. Influenced at first by Korea and China to the west, Japan went on to develop its own distinctive culture and religion.

Honshu, the largest island, lies at the heart of the Japanese archipelago. Hokkaido, the next biggest island, sits to the north. The smaller islands of Shikoku and Kyushu lie southwest of Honshu, across the Inland Sea.

The archipelago forms an arc that stretches 1,200 miles (1,900 km) from north to south. Because of this huge distance, the Japanese islands have very different climates and vegetation. Hokkaido has long, freezing winters and subarctic vegetation. Kyushu has a subtropical climate with lush vegetation.

Inland, most of Japan is occupied by steep mountains covered with dense forests. The only flat land lies near the coasts. In ancient times, settlements grew up only in coastal areas. Travelers crossed between islands by boat.

Because travel was restricted, the people of each island developed widely different traditions and lifestyles.

Early settlers

The first settlers from the Asian mainland arrived in Japan around 30,000 B.C. By 10,000 B.C., the first civilization, called the

Like many peaks in Japan, Mount Fuji is a sacred site that is regarded as the dwelling place of spirits.

This outdoor temple stands beside a volcanic hot spring, another sacred place.

Jomon culture, was developing on the coast of Honshu. The first Jomon were hunter-gatherers who worshipped the spirits of springs, rivers, crags, and other natural features. These beliefs developed into Shinto, Japan's indigenous religion.

After 300 B.C., new settlers from China and Korea showed the Jomon how to grow rice and introduced what is called the Yayoi culture. The first villages grew up, and Japan became a network of small states, ruled by clan chiefs. By the fifth century A.D., one clan, the Yamato, had grown more powerful than all others. Their descendants became emperors of Japan (see pages 44–45).

When Jomon people gave up hunting, they settled as farmers in huts like these.

Izanagi Visits the Underworld

Izanami's last child was Kagutsuchi, the god of fire. In giving birth to him, the goddess was so badly burned that she died and was sent to live in Yomi, the dark, gloomy underworld.

Izanagi was overcome with grief at his wife's death and blamed his newborn son, Kagutsuchi, for causing her to die. He took a sword and cut off the baby's head. Immediately several new gods and goddesses emerged from Kagutsuchi's body. On realizing the horrible thing he had done, Izanagi cried harder than ever. From his tears grew more deities.

When Izanami died, her spirit went to Yomi, the underworld kingdom of the dead. Izanagi decided to journey to the underworld kingdom to bring her back. The god traveled deep into Yomi before he found Izanami's spirit. He explained to her that he was there to take her home, but she said that she could not return to the land of the living because she had eaten the food of the dead. Only the God of Death could release her.

Izanagi vowed to enter the dark hall of the God of Death to plead with him to release his beloved wife's spirit. Although Izanami's spirit urged her husband not to enter the hall, Izanagi paid no attention.

Izanagi marched into the hall but could not see his way through the darkness. Using one of the teeth from his hair comb, he made a flaming torch that shone light everywhere. Immediately screams of death boomed throughout the hall, and he found himself standing over a decaying corpse. It was the lifeless body of Izanami. Izanagi recoiled in horror and fled the hall.

Abandoned and humiliated, Izanami's spirit sent demons, called the hags of Yomi, chasing after Izanagi. With the hags hot on his heels, Izanagi threw down first his headdress, which turned into grapes,

This nineteenth-century painting shows the God of Death sitting on his throne in Yomi, overseeing the horrors of the afterlife.

and then his comb, which became bamboo shoots. Each time the hags stopped to eat the food, Izanagi got farther ahead.

Near the entrance to Yomi, Izanami's spirit changed into one of the hags and came screaming toward him. Izanagi rolled a huge boulder against the entrance to seal it forever.

The Three Greatest Gods

Back in the land of the living, Izanagi felt polluted by the dust of Yomi. He stripped off his clothes and washed in the Hi River. Each time he scrubbed off some of the dust, a new deity was born.

When he washed his face, he gave birth to the three greatest deities. Washing his left eye, Izanagi gave birth to Amaterasu, the sun goddess. The moon god, Tsuki-yomi, came from Izanagi's right eye. The storm god, Susano-wo, came from Izanagi's nose.

Now Izanagi divided the universe between his three new children. He gave the eldest, Amaterasu, five strings of jewels and rule over the heavens. He made Susano-wo the god of the oceans, and he gave Tsuki-yomi the kingdom of the night.

Religion in Japan

Shinto, Confucianism, and Buddhism have been practiced in Japan for centuries. Shinto, which originated in Japan, was influenced by the other two religions, which came from Asia.

A Shinto priestess performs ritual prayers to the *kami* at a shrine in Japan.

Traditionally, the Japanese are a very devout and religious people. Until 1945, Shinto was the official religion in Japan. Shinto, a name that means "the way of the gods," is a very ancient religion, dating back thousands of years to Jomon times (see page 29). The main Shinto deities are Izanagi's children: Amaterasu, Tsuki-yomi, and Susano-wo (see pages 30–31). In addition to these and other major figures, there are literally millions of lesser deities called *kami* ("spirits").

Snow-capped mountains, rivers, seas, ancient trees, and other natural wonders all contain *kami*. The Japanese believed that all people, from shoguns to peasants, became *kami* when they died.

The Japanese built shrines up and down the country for regular worship of their deities. Entering a shrine through a ceremonial gateway called a *torii*, worshippers wash to purify themselves before praying, just as Izanagi did after leaving Yomi.

There are two main groups of *kami*, heavenly and earthly spirits. Originally, the gods moved freely between heaven and earth, but after the bridge between the two places collapsed into the sea, the spirits stuck on earth remained there. All *kami* are essentially good, but they have two souls, one gentle and the other violent. They can bring disaster and misfortune if their violent soul gets the upper hand, so they have to be appeased through prayer.

Shinto encourages respect for nature and reverence for, even worship of, one's ancestors. It also stresses the importance of ritual and tradition.

This ninth-century *torii* gate marks the sacred entrance to a Shinto shrine at Miyajima.

Other Beliefs

As well as Shinto, Confucianism and Buddhism are important religions in Japan, both having spread to the islands from mainland Asia. Buddhism became popular in Japan in the sixth century A.D., having arrived from Korea. It has been practiced side by side with Shintoism ever since. In medieval times, Zen Buddhism, a form of Buddhism that stresses the importance of meditation, became popular among the samurai (the warrior class).

Arriving in Japan around the same time as Buddhism, Confucianism greatly influenced the more mystical Shinto. Today, most Japanese people practice a mix of the major religions. They perform Shinto at births and marriages and Buddhist ceremonies at funerals.

SOURCES OF JAPANESE MYTHS

The stories about Izanagi and his three children, Amaterasu, Tsuki-yomi, and Susano-wo, are very ancient. Before the Japanese developed a written script, these and other myths were handed down by word of mouth. At the beginning of the eighth century A.D., Empress Gemmyo commissioned scholars to produce a written anthology of Shinto legends and a history of Japan. The anthology, entitled *Kojiki* ("The Record of Ancient Matters"), was completed in 712, and the *Nihon Shoki* ("Chronicles of Japan") in 720. The books are the main sources of Japanese myths.

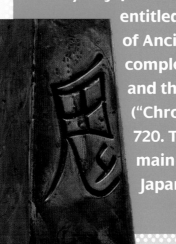

Amaterasu Hides the Daylight

Amaterasu and Tsuki-yomi settled down to rule the realms of day and night, as their father, Izanagi, had ordered. Only Susano-wo, the storm god, was unhappy with his realm. He set out to stir up trouble among his siblings.

Susano-wo, the god of storms, climbed to Takamagahara, or the High Plain of Heaven, where his father, Izanagi, had been raised (see page 26). There he challenged his sister, Amaterasu, the sun goddess, to a miracle-working contest. Amaterasu took her brother's sword, broke it into three pieces, and used them to create three goddesses. In reply, Susano-wo took Amaterasu's five strings of jewels and used them to create five male deities.

Susano-wo was sure he had done enough to win the competition. When it was declared a draw, he was angry and frustrated. He became wild and destructive. He summoned storms and wrecked the rice fields that his sister had planted on earth. Amaterasu fled in terror and shut herself up in a rocky cave.

Amaterasu's disappearance plunged the earth into darkness and perpetual winter. For a long time she refused to budge. Eventually the sound of the other gods singing and laughing at the antics of Ama-no-Uzume, a dawn goddess, tempted Amaterasu to look out of the cave. There she caught sight of her own reflection in a magic mirror.

The End of a Dark Period

Mistaking her image for a rival sun goddess, Amaterasu stepped outside to take a closer look. As soon as she did so, the other gods seized her and roped off the cave so she could not get inside again. Reluctantly, Amaterasu agreed to return to the realm of heaven. In this way, sunlight and life-giving warmth were restored to the world.

In Japanese religion, Susano-wo, the god of storms, is just as important as his sister, Amaterasu, the sun goddess.

Farming in Japan

Amaterasu, the Shinto sun goddess, is the principal deity in Japanese mythology. Her status reflects the importance of the sun and its effect on a good harvest.

Amaterasu is worshipped all over Japan. Her main shrine is at Ise in central Honshu. Considering that the sun goddess is the primary deity in Shinto mythology, it may seem surprising that her main shrine is a simple wooden structure shaped like a grain store. Yet the shape of the building serves as a reminder of the sun's importance in producing much-needed crops for food.

The Japanese abandoned hunting and gathering in around 300 B.C. and settled down to farming. One of the main crops they grew was rice. Other important crops included wheat, millet, red beans, and soybeans. Vegetables, such as radishes and sweet potatoes, and many types of fruit were also grown.

Growing Rice

Rice cultivation requires moist conditions and intensive farming methods. The crop was often grown in flooded fields called rice paddies, where carp fish were also kept for food. All over Japan, hillsides were cut into terraces to make maximum use of the small amount of land that could be farmed—much of the country is too steep and mountainous for agriculture of this kind. In spring,

Traditional farmhouses stand beside a rice field in Shirakawa-go, a carefully maintained heritage site in western Honshu, Japan.

Mount Fuji is reflected in the water of this paddy as a Japanese farm worker plants rice by hand.

farmers painstakingly planted neat rows of rice seedlings on the muddy terraces. Whole families stood knee-deep in cold water for long hours to carry out this backbreaking work.

Farmers in Society

As in China, farmers were respected but lived a hard life. Most peasants did not own the land they worked but rented it from landlords. A large part of their harvest went straight to the landlord in tax, and they were not free to leave the land. This situation continued, more or less, into the nineteenth century, when it was virtually abolished. After World War II

(1939–1945), further land reforms were introduced, and many more farmers were able to buy land.

Japanese society was traditionally divided into four main classes. The samurai, or warrior class, had the highest status. Next came farmers who produced food, and craftsmen who made useful tools and weapons. Merchants were considered the lowest class because they did not actually produce anything. That social order changed in the twentieth century, when many merchants in Japan became richer than farmers because they made bigger profits through trade.

Susano-wo and the Dragon's Sword

Although Susano-wo was the god of storms and thunder, he was not always wicked. In this myth, he rids the world of an evil dragon and discovers a magical sword that would later be prized by the emperors of Japan.

The other gods punished Susano-wo for his poor treatment of Amaterasu, which had forced the sun goddess to take refuge in a cave (see page 34). The gods cut off the storm god's beard, pulled out his toenails and fingernails, and banished him from heaven.

Forced to wander the earth, Susano-wo traveled alone for many years until, in the Izumo region of western Japan, he met an elderly couple and their young daughter, Kusa-nada-Hime. All three were weeping. When Susano-wo asked what was wrong, the old man told him that Kusa-nada-Hime was the only survivor of their eight daughters. The other seven girls had been killed by a terrible dragon called Yamata-no-Orochi. The dragon, which had eight heads and eight tails, had only been hunting in the region for a few days. Now their last child was about to be killed by the dragon, too.

Susano-wo told the couple that he was the brother of Amaterasu, the sun goddess. In recognition of his importance, the couple promised to give him their daughter if he could defeat the dragon. Susano-wo prepared eight huge vats of sake (rice wine) and settled down to wait for Yamata-no-Orochi. When the dragon appeared, the smell of the wine drew it straight to the vats, and all eight heads drank deeply. The dragon quickly became drunk and fell into a deep sleep.

Slaying the Dragon

Susano-wo saw his chance and cut off all eight of the dragon's heads. Then he cut the dragon's body into pieces and chopped up the eight tails. In one of the

This colorful carved dragon sits on the roof of a Shinto temple in Yokohama City, Japan.

dragon's middle tails, he found a gleaming, magical sword that would later feature in many legends.

The sword would be called Kusanagi, which means "the grass-mower," because of an adventure in which a hero used it to cut down the high grass that was hiding his enemy. Over the following years, Kusanagi's fame grew, and the sword became one of the emblems of the Japanese emperors. It is now said to be housed in a temple near the town of Nagoya in central Honshu.

As for Susano-wo, he married Kusa-nada-Hime, and the couple moved into a palace near the town of Suga. There they lived happily, and Kusa-nada-Hime gave birth to a daughter, Suseri-Hime.

Swords and Samurai

The many adventures of the dragon's sword, known as Kusanagi, show how highly the Japanese prized swords. This was especially true for the samurai, the elite warrior class that emerged in medieval times.

During the medieval period, Japan's most powerful clans waged war almost constantly. Clan chiefs called *daimyo* hired armies of samurai—the word means "one who serves"—to fight on their behalf.

By the twelfth century, the samurai had developed a complex code of conduct called bushido, which means "the way of the warrior." The code placed a warrior's honor above life itself. Instead of conceding defeat, a samurai would commit seppuku (ritual suicide) by first slicing open his own belly before another samurai ended his agony by cutting off his head.

In battle, the samurai wore heavy armor made of strips of metal and leather bound together with silk. Their helmets bore terrifying emblems designed to frighten their enemies. Originally, the samurai fought mainly on horseback, using bows and arrows. Later they became expert swordsmen. Only members of the warrior class were allowed to carry the long, curved swords called *katana*.

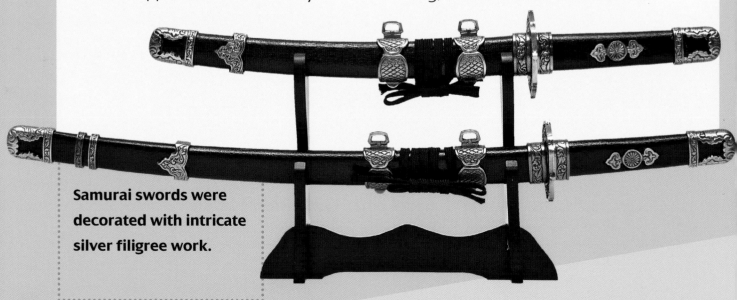

Samurai swords were decorated with intricate silver filigree work.

Forging the Sword

A samurai's sword was his most prized possession. The finest weapons were precious heirlooms, handed down from father to son. A samurai sword took hours of painstaking work to make, as the metal blade was coated with many thin layers of steel and then honed to razor-sharpness. The smiths who produced the weapons were master craftsmen, and their work took on a spiritual dimension. Before starting a sword, the smith would fast to purify himself, as if embarking on a religious quest.

In the seventeenth century, wars became less frequent. The samurai adapted their fighting skills into ritual arts and became more interested in peaceful pursuits than in mortal combat. Despite its benevolent activities, the samurai class was abolished in the late nineteenth century.

This nineteenth-century painting shows a medieval battle between samurai warriors.

Samurai dress was decorative as well as protective.

Okuninushi and Ninigi

Legends claim that the province of Izumo in western Japan had several famous rulers. One was Okuninushi, the god of medicine and healing. Another was Ninigi, whose descendants became emperors of Japan.

Okuninushi had 80 brothers who were all jealous of him, and once he had grown, they tried to kill him. Once he narrow brush with death, the young man decided to take refuge in the village of Suga. There he met and fell in love with Suseri-Hime, daughter of Susano-wo, the storm god, and Kusa-nada-Hime.

Suseri-Hime was kind and invited the stranger to sleep at her family's palace. Susano-wo was suspicious of Okuninushi and set a series of traps to get rid of the unwelcome suitor.

On the first night of his stay, Susano-wo made Okuninushi sleep in a room filled with poisonous snakes. He spent the second night in a room full of wasps and centipedes. Suseri-Hime gave Okuninushi a magic scarf that protected him from harm on both occasions.

Another time, Susano-wo sent Okuninushi into the middle of a giant meadow to fetch an arrow, then set fire to the grass. Okuninushi was saved by a mouse that retrieved the arrow and showed him an underground chamber where he could hide from the flames.

Escape to Freedom

Okuninushi decided to steal away with Suseri-Hime. One night, when Susano-wo was asleep, Okuninushi tied the storm god's hair to the rafters and then escaped with Suseri-Hime. Susano-wo woke up and, while trying to release himself, pulled down the whole palace. He emerged from the rubble and pursued the fleeing couple, but the young lovers managed to escape.

Far away from Suga, Okuninushi and Suseri-Hime married and settled down to rule the kingdom of Izumo. Okuninushi's brothers, who were still jealous, waged war on him, and their realm was reduced to chaos.

Amaterasu, the sun goddess, then intervened and placed her own grandson, Ninigi, on the throne of Izumo.

Okuninushi was forced to abdicate when Ninigi appeared bearing three divine gifts that proved he was Amaterasu's grandson. The gifts were the heavenly jewels, the mirror that the gods had used to lure Amaterasu from the cave (see page 34), and the sword later named Kusanagi (see page 39). These three treasures later became the symbols of Japanese imperial power.

Founding a Dynasty

Ninigi married the daughter of a mountain god, but when his young wife became pregnant not long after the wedding, he suspected her of being unfaithful.

The young bride was determined to prove her innocence. When the time came for her to give birth, she shut herself inside a house without doors or windows and then set fire to it, declaring that she would die if she had been unfaithful. Instead of being burned to death, she survived and bore triplets, all three of whom were boys. One of the boys became the founder of the Yamato imperial line of Japan.

The Imperial Palace in Tokyo has been the official residence of the Japanese emperors since they moved there from Kyoto in 1868.

The Emperors of Japan

The Yamato family have sat on the imperial throne of Japan for over 1,500 years. Yet for many centuries, they were forced to be subservient to the families that controlled the office of shogun.

When the Yamato family began their long, warring conquest of Japan around A.D. 330, the country was made up of rival clans and small states. The wars finally ended in the fifth century with the unification of the country and the beginning of the Yamato imperial line.

Historians believe that the myth of Ninigi taking the Izumo throne from Okuninushi (see pages 42–43) is based on the ancient victory of the Yamato clan over its rivals. The Yamato worshipped Amaterasu, the sun goddess, while their main rivals paid homage to Susano-wo, the god of storms and the sea. After their victory, the Yamato clan made Amaterasu the principal deity of the new empire. They also claimed her as their own ancestor.

From that time on, Japanese emperors were regarded as living gods, descendants of the sun

Many Japanese banknotes carry portraits of historical rulers and sacred sites.

goddess. In recognition of their divine ancestor, the rising sun became the national emblem. It still appears on the Japanese flag.

Emperor as God

As in China, the Japanese emperor was believed to have a mandate from heaven and was considered a living deity. When the emperor appeared in public, ordinary people were supposed to hide indoors or bow down low enough to avoid looking at his face.

Following Japan's defeat in World War II (1939–1945), Emperor Hirohito (1901–1989) was forced by the Allies to declare that he was not a living god. Today the emperor's role is largely ceremonial, similar to that of European monarchs.

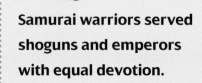

Samurai warriors served shoguns and emperors with equal devotion.

THE SHOGUN VERSUS THE EMPEROR

Although the imperial period stretches back 1,500 years, for most of that time Japan was governed by military leaders called shoguns, who took over from the emperors in the twelfth century. During the thirteenth century, the Minamoto clan ruled Japan as shoguns. They were followed by the Ashikaga shogunate (1338–1573). From 1603 to 1868, the title was held by the Tokugawa family. The Emperor Meiji finally reasserted imperial control over Japan in 1868.

Glossary

Ama-no-Uzume In Japanese mythology, a dawn goddess who lured Amaterasu out of her cave, restoring sunlight to the world.

Amaterasu In Japan, the sun goddess, the supreme Shinto deity. She was the daughter of Izanagi.

Buddhism An ancient Indian religion that spread to China and Japan. It teaches a belief in reincarnation and that its followers should lead virtuous lives.

bushido Samurai code of conduct that emphasized honor above one's own life.

Cheng (259–210 B.C.) Chinese emperor who began the Great Wall of China. Also called Shih Huang-ti.

Confucianism An ancient Chinese belief system, founded by K'ung Fu-tzu (551–479 B.C.), also known as Confucius, that teaches, among other things, the importance of tradition.

Di Jun In Chinese mythology, a god who had 10 sons, each a sun.

Gemmyo An eighth-century Japanese empress who ordered the documenting of Shinto legends.

Gonggong In Chinese mythology, the god of water who tried to destroy humans by flooding the earth.

Gun The god who tried to stop Gonggong from flooding the earth.

Hiruko The first son of Izanagi and Izanami. He was born a leech child and abandoned by his parents. He survived and became known as Ebisu, the god of fishermen and good fortune.

Izanagi Father of Japan, husband to Izanami, and creator of the three major deities, Amaterasu, Tsuki-yomi, and Susano-wo.

Izanami Wife to Izanagi and mother of Japan. She died giving birth to Kagutsuchi.

Izumo Province in western Japan from where the imperial family, Yamato, emerged.

Jomon Japan's first civilization, which began around 10,000 B.C.

junk A large seafaring ship.

kami In Shinto religion, the lesser gods, who include the spirits of ancestors. They exist in inanimate objects such as rocks, trees, rivers, and streams.

Kusa-nada-Hime In Japanese mythology, the wife of Susano-wo and the mother of Suseri-Hime.

Kusanagi The sword pulled out of the tail of the dragon Yamata-no-Orochi; an emblem of the Japanese emperors.

Lao-tzu The founder of Taoism in the sixth century B.C.

Ninigi Grandson of Amaterasu and ancestor of the Yamato dynasty.

Nu Wa In Chinese mythology, the goddess, half serpent and half woman, who created humans.

Okuninushi Husband of Suseri-Hime and ruler of Izumo province before Ninigi.

Onogoro The first island created by Izanagi and Izanami. Its exact location is disputed.

Pan Ku In Chinese mythology, a giant who created the yin (earth) and the yang (heavens).

sampan Small wooden Chinese boat.

samurai Japanese elite warriors or mercenaries.

seppuku A type of ritual suicide performed by samurai.

Shinto An ancient Japanese belief system. The religion encourages respect for nature and one's ancestors.

shoguns Military leaders who held the real power in Japan from the twelfth century to the nineteenth century.

Susano-wo The storm god and son of Izanagi. He forced his sister, Amaterasu, into a cave and defeated the dragon Yamata-no-Orochi.

Suseri-Hime The daughter of Susano-wo, she married Okuninushi and ruled Izumo with him before Ninigi.

Takamagahara Also known as the High Plain of Heaven, it was where Izanagi and Izanami were raised. It was also the place from where Amaterasu ruled the heavens.

Taoism An ancient Chinese mystical religion that teaches its followers to strive for perfection through harmony with nature.

Tiandi In Chinese mythology, a chief god who ordered Gonggong to flood the world.

T'ien Hou In Chinese mythology, a young girl whose spirit saved sailors from drowning. She is also known as the Empress of Heaven.

torii The ceremonial gateway to a Shinto shrine.

Tsuki-yomi The moon god and son of Izanagi.

Wu Di An ancient Chinese emperor who declared the importance of agriculture.

Xi He In Chinese mythology, the wife of Di Jun.

Xi Wangmu The wife of Yu Huang, she was also called the Queen Mother of the West.

Yamata-no-Orochi In Japanese mythology, the terrible dragon that was killed by Susano-wo.

Yamato The imperial family of Japan. They are believed to be descended from Amaterasu and Ninigi, and have ruled Japan for over 1,500 years.

Yao In Chinese mythology, an ancient emperor who pleaded with the gods to save the world.

Yayoi The Japanese civilization, which began in China and Korea, that overtook the Jomon around 300 B.C.

Yi In Chinese mythology, the divine archer who shot down nine of the 10 suns and saved the crops.

yin and yang The essence of the universe, with the earth being yin and the heavens, yang. It is believed that these two forces are equal and that, when joined together, they create a balanced harmony.

Yomi In Japanese mythology, the underworld.

Yu In Chinese mythology, the son of Gun and the one who stopped Gonggong from flooding the earth.

Yu Huang Also known as the Jade Emperor, the ruler of the heavens and chief god in the Chinese pantheon.

Zen Buddhism A form of Buddhism that emphasizes mental meditation. It is popular in Japan and in many other places around the world.

Zheng He A fifteenth-century Chinese admiral who explored as far as the east coast of Africa.

Further Information

BOOKS

Cass, Victoria Baldwin. *In the Realm of the Gods: Lands, Myths, and Legends of China*. San Francisco, CA: Long River Press, 2007.

Storm, Rachel. *Mythology of Asia and the Far East: Myths and Legends of China, Japan, Thailand, Malaysia, and Indonesia*. London, England: Southwater, 2006.

VIDEOS

Religions: Shinto. Schlessinger Media, 1999.

Touring China. Questar, 1998.

WEB SITES

Japanese Myths
  http://www.st.rim.or.jp/~cycle/myrefE.HTML

Japanese Mythology
  http://www.interq.or.jp/www-user/fuushi/e-myth-a.htm

Selected Chinese Myths and Fantasies
  http://www.chinavista.com/experience/story/story.html

Index

Page numbers in *italics* refer to picture captions

agriculture 16
Ama-no-Uzume 34
Amaterasu 5, 31, 32, 33, 34, *35*, 36, 38, 42, 43, 44
Ashikaga 45

Beijing *13*
Buddha *5*
Buddhism 5, 8, 9, 32, 33
bushido 40

Cheng *see* Yangtze River
Ch'in dynasty 12
Chuang Tzu 9
Confucianism 5, 8, 9, 32, 33
Confucius *4*, 8

daimyo 40
Di Jun 14

Ebisu 27
Empress of Heaven 22–23
endless wheel 20

farmers 16–17
Fuji, Mount *28*, *37*

Gemmyo 33
God of Death 30, *31*
Gonggong 18
Grand Canal 21
Great Wall 12, *13*
Gun 18

Han 8
Han dynasty 12
Hi River 31
Hirohito 45
Hiruko 27
Hokkaido 28
Honshu 28, 29, 36, 39
Huang Ho *see* Yellow River

imperial palace, Beijing *13*
imperial palace, Tokyo *43*
Inland Sea 28
Ise 36
Izanagi 26–27, 30–31, 32, 33, 34
Izanami 26–27, 30, 31
Izumo 42, 44

Jade Emperor 5, 10–11, 12, 22
Jomon 29, 32
junks 24, 25

Kagutsuchi 30
Kamakura, Japan *5*
kami 5, 32
karma 9
katana 40
Kojiki 33
Korea *7*, 29, 33
K'uei Hsing 11
K'ung Fu-tzu *see* Confucius
Kusa-nada-Hime 38, 39, 42
Kusanagi 39, 40, 43
Kyushu 28

Lao-tzu 10

magnetic compass 25
Marco Polo 25
Mei-chou 22
Meiji 45
Middle Kingdom 8
Minamoto 45
Ming dynasty 9
Miyajima *33*

Nagoya 39
Nihon Shoki 33
Ninigi 42–43, 44
Nu Wa 6, 8

Okuninushi 42–43, 44
Onogoro 26

paddies 36, *37*
Pan Ku 6

Qi 19
Qing dynasty 13
Quan Yin *9*

rice *16*, 17, 36, 37
Romance of the Investiture of the Gods 9

sake 38
sampan 24
samurai 33, 40, 41, *45*
seppuku 40
Shang dynasty 12
Shih Huang-ti 12
Shikoku 28
Shinto 5, 29, 32, 33, 36
Shirakawa-go *36*
shoguns 32, 45
Song dynasty 13
Suga 42
Sui dynasty 13, 21
Susano-wo 31, 32, 33, 34, *35*, 38–39, 42, 44
Suseri-Hime 39, 42

Takamagahara 26, 34
Tang dynasty 13
Taoism 5, 8, 9, 10
Tao-te Ching 9
terra-cotta army *12*
Three Gorges dam 21
Tiandi 18
T'ien Hou 22–23, 24
Tokugawa 45
torii 32, *33*
Travels in the West 9
Tsuki-yomi 31, 32, 33, 34

Wu Di 16

Xi He 14
Xi Wangmu 10, 15

Yamata-no-Orochi 38
Yamato 29, 43, 44
Yangtze River 8, 13, 20, 21
Yao 14, 18
Yayoi 29
Yellow River 6, 8, 13, 20, 21
Yi 14–15, 18
yin and yang 6, *7*, 9
Yomi 30, 31, 32
Yong Le 25
Yu 18, 19
Yu Huang Shang-di 10
Yuan dynasty 13

Zen Buddhism 33
Zhang E 15
Zheng, Admiral 25
Zhong-guo 8
Zhou dynasty 12